IN THE HEARTBEAT OF THE PAUSE,
WE DISCOVER THE STRENGTH
TO EMBRACE EACH MOMENT,
TRANSFORMING PRESENCE INTO
THE CORNERSTONE OF OUR
UNDERSTANDING OF LOSS.

M.C.Bell.

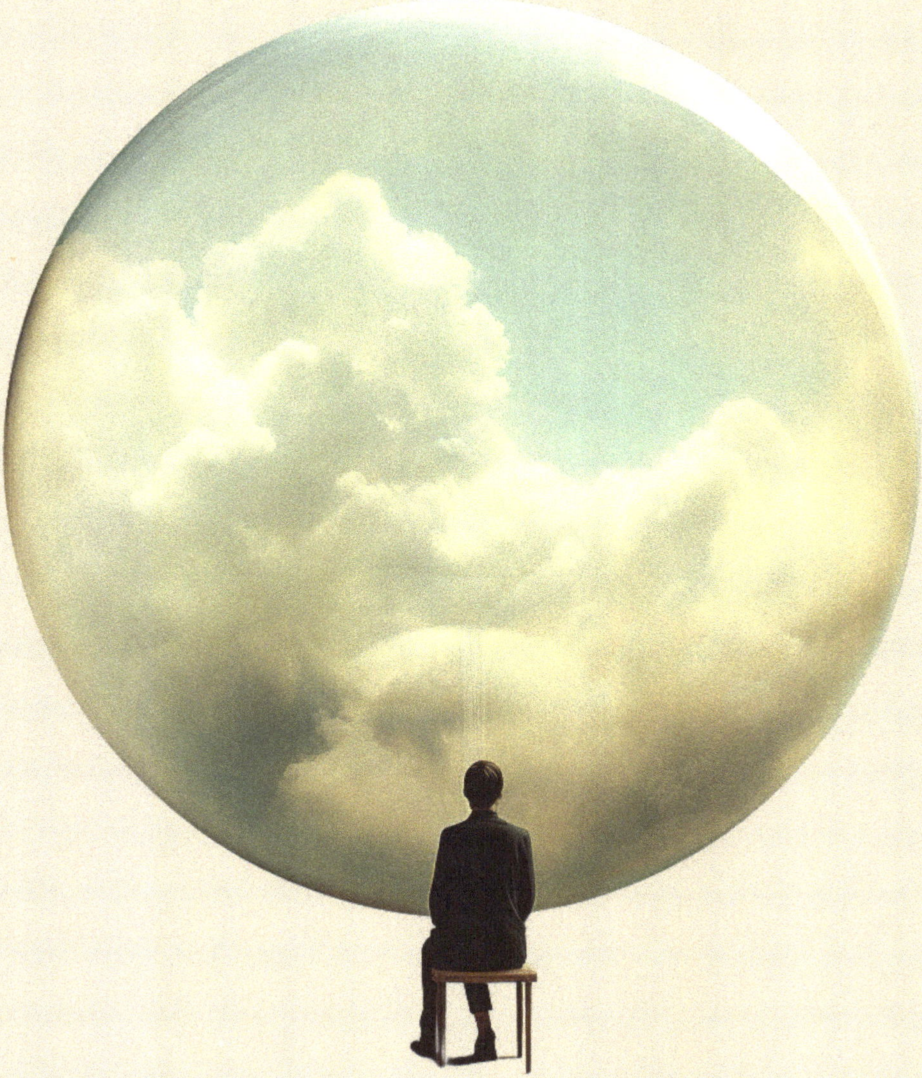

I have been blessed to know Michele—a woman of unshakable spirit, dignity, and beauty.

In facing life's formidable challenges, Michele has crafted a world resplendent with beauty and resilience. Her path, marked by the single-handed upbringing of her children, has been interwoven with a profound dedication to healing and inspiring others. This journey transcends the traditional confines of a career, embodying instead a vocation pursued with unmatched passion and purpose. Her creativity is limitless, merging effortlessly with an intuitive wisdom that has provided solace and direction to many.

Michele's commitment to imparting her knowledge and energy elevates her contributions far beyond the ordinary, rendering her teachings a treasure for those seeking enlightenment and transformative change. Her loyalty to the upliftment of others is profound, positioning her as an invaluable guide for anyone navigating the intricacies of life and seeking healing. I wholeheartedly endorse Michele's works and teachings to anyone drawn to a journey of significant, soulful discovery—her influence is a remarkable gift to the world, unparalleled in its depth and scope.

– JULIAN LAMPERT, Classical Pianist

Foundation of
EMBRACE

Prelude to Stage Three

This foundational section provides a comprehensive overview of *The 7 Stages of Grief*, setting the stage for the deep dive into **Be Present** that follows. While it serves as an introduction, it is designed to be revisited, offering insight and context as you navigate through each stage of your journey.

The EMBRACE Journey
Transform Grief and
Discover Inner *Strength*

Welcome, Warriors, to the extraordinary dimension of the 7 Stages of Grief Workbook Journal. I will guide you through a miraculous and empowering passage, unveiling the hidden treasures amidst the labyrinth of trauma and loss.

This course was born from my authentic desire to *heal it forward* in the grief community, ignited by theta meditation and a deep desire to manifest growth and healing through my writings. Drawing upon my intuitive theta-visions, I have created the EMBRACE framework — a radiant constellation of seven stages illuminating our transformative expedition in the wake of adversity.

In contrast to conventional approaches that merely skim the surface of emotions within the limited confines of the five stages of grief, I sensed the dire need for a holistic and transformative tapestry. The 7 stages of grief, meticulously crafted through my Healing it Forward modalities used in my 1:1 sacred retreats, transcend the ephemeral realm of emotions, ushering us into a realm where storytelling, the sacred utterance of our beloved's name, and the cultivation of gratitude mingle, guiding us through each challenging obstacle that graces our path.

Within this cherished community of kindred souls, we will unite, bound by a shared mission to collaborate, share our truth, and breathe life into one another's spirits—a sacred alchemy that fosters a radiant cascade of healing and metamorphosis. The modalities unveiled in the EMBRACE workbook journal's resplendent pages revolutionized how we navigate our sacred inner landscape, transforming the lives of those who have an unwavering longing to embrace the transformative work ahead.

As an extraordinary boon, I invite you to journey beside me as a Certified Grief Wellness Warrior, armed with the profound and purposeful modalities needed to extend a gentle hand to those ensnared in the clutches of their grief. By immersing yourself in these transformative practices and obtaining certification, you shall illuminate the path for others in their darkest moments, serving as a beacon of light and hope amidst the unfathomable abyss.

With deepest gratitude and genuine admiration, I extend my heartfelt appreciation to you for summoning the courage to embark upon the sacred journey of the EMBRACE workbook journal course. I assure you, Warriors, that this decision shall cascade with blessings and profoundly resonate. Together, let us traverse the infinite depths of grief, unlocking the wellspring of our inner fortitude and embarking upon a journey that transcends healing alone—a voyage brimming with purpose, renewal, and the willful power of the human spirit.

Prepare yourself for the transformational power of the 7 Stages of Grief Workbook Journal.

Let our extraordinary odyssey begin.

The Grief Warrior

Table of Contents

FOREWARD

My name is Cristal Sampson, and I work in mental health and psychiatry as a nurse practitioner in the UK, Connecticut, and New York, specializing in traumatic stress and mood disorders. I am also a young woman who experienced an early-term spontaneous miscarriage that burned a hole in depths I had previously not known existed. The revelation of this new depth of unconditional love, coupled with my baby's teeny heart stopping, left me hollow.

Even in my subsequent pregnancy the following year, I still felt empty of the unfulfillable desire for the baby back that I had lost in this life. The emptiness was filled with sadness, anxiety, and disappointment from troubled family dynamics – *a family unaware of my loss and grief.*

Someone with my expertise is never immune to the heartaches of the human experience, such as the loss of love and life. I recognized the potential to become an emotionally absent mother to my unborn baby, a fate that seemed all but certain at the time – and the thought terrified me. I am grateful to have understood that both my baby and I deserved the opportunity to heal. In my research, I discovered Michele, The Grief Warrior®.

As a health professional and a mental health specialist, I am particularly discerning about the services I opt for and the providers I choose. During this chapter of my life and given the circumstances, I did not pursue "traditional" mental health counseling. At that moment, confronting the challenges presented by contemporary therapy seemed beyond my capacity. I perceived the potential for a more conventional approach to be beneficial later in my healing journey.

What Michele provided touched the very core, breadth, and depth of my pain, reaching deep into the spiritual, mental, emotional, and energetic aspects of my being, body, and environment through a one-on-one retreat. I have not encountered anything like it since. Therefore, I am deeply moved that you are here, exploring the 7 Stages of Grief. Your journey with Michele's intentional energy, as conveyed through her books, and her custom human design modalities coupled with her healing energy, will extensively shift your essence and transform you.

FOREWARD

The 'EMBRACE: The 7 Stages of Grief' workbook series is designed to support every individual navigating grief—those who feel unprepared and overwhelmed by the complexities of losing a loved one. This series speaks to the heart of those oscillating between the anticipation of loss and the necessity of maintaining 'normalcy,' amidst the swirl of anger, resentment, and sorrow. It is a compassionate companion for every silent sufferer, for those caught in the emotional storm of impending loss, and for caregivers in dire need of nurturing themselves.

What distinguishes Michele's 'The 7 Stages of Grief' series most is the infusion of practical hope within its pages—a hope that is both tangible and deeply rooted in the natural spaces where resilience and healing begin. Michele brings a deep understanding and mastery in guiding others through the vast resources available for grief support, offering pathways that are both practical and easily navigable. Her insight into the caregiver journey, as a single mother is profoundly intimate, shaped by her own experience of lovingly supporting her teenage son, through his transition, enveloped in a cocoon of love. This unique perspective enriches her approach, making her guidance not only informed but deeply empathetic to the nuanced experiences of grief.

My work with Michele has caused a seismic shift in my perspective and has improved my relationships with myself, my family, and the people who meet me. I am moved with infinite gratitude at the positive and priceless impact my work with Michele has had on my experience of motherhood and the beautiful relationship my daughter and I get to have. Now, I enjoy expanding my connection as she has become a selfless friend and true mentor.

I encourage you to allow this book to transform you positively. Let it be a daily source of support and comfort, especially in moments of need. Remember, everything Michele has undertaken since Nicky's return to the Source has been a heartfelt ode to him and a homage to the enduring legacy of love and purpose he entrusted to her. Michele's ultimate wish is for you to discover your purpose and allow it to drive you forward through the cherished journey of your life.

Cristal Sampoon

FROM MY HEART
to yours...

Alignment in the face of loss is the only option. When we open ourselves to the possibilities presented to us, we find this harmony: in the strength of our words, in the peace of our meditations, in the gift of our presence, in the renewal of our bodies, in the stirring of our spirits, in the depth of our relationships, and in the nourishment we give ourselves.

The path to recovery is a beautiful tapestry that offers the opportunity for personal development and the forging of inner fortitude. We will brave new territory together, learn new things, and grow as people. I will be your guide and source of solace throughout our journey together. Get ready to reclaim your life with renewed confidence as you learn to swiftly navigate life's complications and unleash your remarkable inner potential.

There is nothing scary or complicated about this course since I will be there to guide you through every one of the steps. Let's take off on a journey into the unknown, where the payoff to SELF could be infinite.

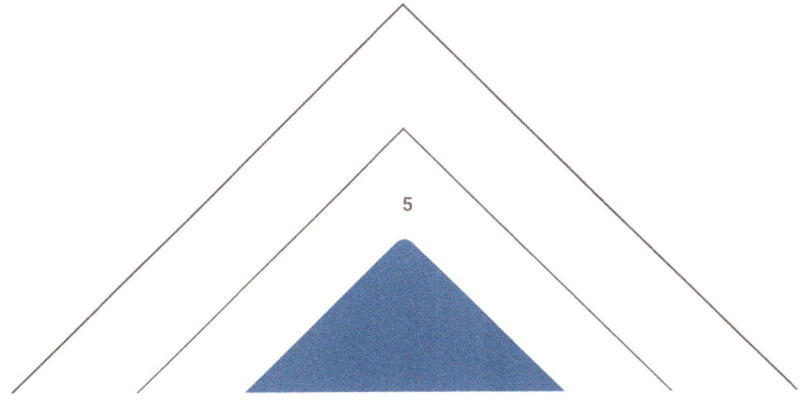

PROLONGED GRIEF DISORDER Unveiled
as total B.S

Shattering the Illusion: Liberating Ourselves from the Constraints of the "5 Stages of Grief"

Adhering to established norms is a delusion, a fallacy we must quickly let go of when dealing with extended grief disorder. The "5 Stages of Bereavement" model developed by psychologists has been widely disseminated for too long, permeating every aspect of grief counseling and education.

Unfortunately, the constant push to conform to a set and narrow path of grieving has led me and countless other seekers within the grief community to feel disillusioned.

I beg you to disregard this erroneous advice immediately. The core meaning of our name, "EMBRACE," contains the whole truth. The concept of "Prolonged Grief Disorder" is 100% bogus.

The "5 Stages of Grief" concept originated from an unsupported theory meant to characterize the reaction of people who had been given fatal diagnoses rather than those who were navigating the maze of loss and sorrow. Here we have two utterly dissimilar yet actual experiences, each of which calls for special attention and comprehension.

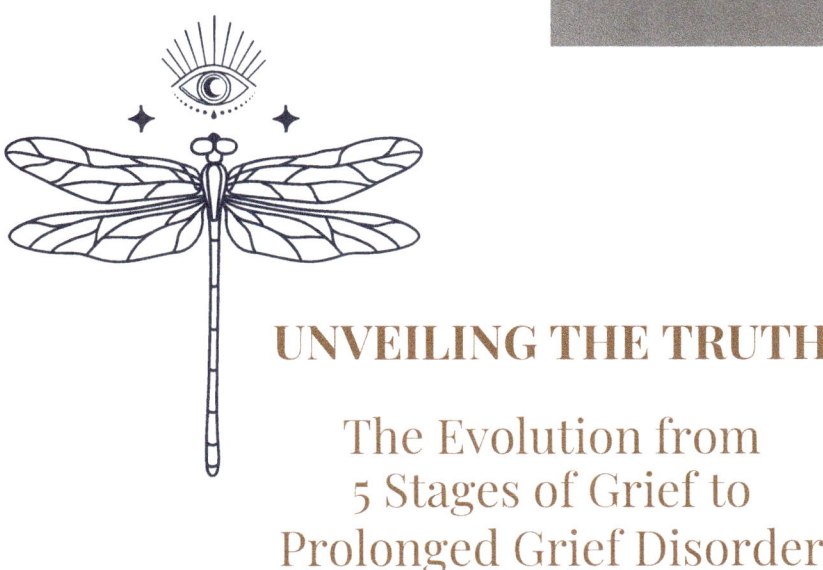

UNVEILING THE TRUTH

The Evolution from 5 Stages of Grief to Prolonged Grief Disorder

In March 2022, a new grief-related disorder was officially adopted into mainstream mental health diagnosis nomenclature. Seeing how the clinical world has further shamed the sacred grieving world is disheartening. DSM-5's trauma and stress-related category have a new label: Prolonged Grief Disorder, created deliberately to define what grief should and should not look like.

But first, let's take a moment to think. What exactly is this thing called "Prolonged Grief Disorder"? Claiming a year for adults and a paltry six months for children is an arrogant attempt to restrict the complex fabric of grief inside the confines of time. According to the American Psychological Association, persons who carry this label are assumed to exhibit the following symptoms even after the diagnostic window has closed:

- The crushing weight of grief pressed down on every aspect of their being.
- An unending fixation on sorrow as memories of the lost reverberate ceaselessly.
- A mental panorama obscured by agony or the unsettling absence of feeling.
- They engage in a delicate dance of denial and avoidance as they try to face their loved one's death.
- Dissonance and disconnection can develop when one feels different from the social norm.
- Every breath is filled with the haunting repercussions of despair and isolation.

We stand at the intersection of societal, cultural, and religious expectations, where the mere fulfillment of established criteria has become pivotal in making a prognosis. Understandably, when engulfed by the darkness of losing a loved one, such clinical classifications may not bring the peace and comprehension one wants.

To promote genuine healing, we need to permit ourselves to explore our inner emotional landscape freely.

Let us stand up as one in our resolve to overcome this stereotype's obstacles. Let us regain our freedom from societal norms to grieve and heal as we see fit.

We will overcome obstacles as a group and EMBRACE the journey of getting to the heart of our pain and reclaiming our ways forward in healing.

WHY PROLONGED GRIEF DISORDER
is Facing So Much Criticism

01

There is no moral compass in the arena of mourning.

Grief isn't reducible to a single feeling but incorporates many of them. It weaves a complex and ever-changing mosaic of emotions, including sadness, rage, anguish, loneliness, reverence, connection, and perplexity.

It's a shared adventure that everyone does on their terms.

Grief is complex and multifaceted: No two souls mourn alike, for no two losses are identical. Attempts to confine the grieving process within cookie-cutter stages, rigid criteria, and prescribed timelines propagate the fallacy of a right or wrong way to grieve.

02

Grief, in its essence, is a natural phenomenon—

A sacred dance that unfolds within the depths of our being. It is a deeply personal and profound experience, far from being a pathological problem to be solved.

A child's heart carries the imprint of a parent's absence for months or years. Similarly, a parent's longing for a child, partner, or loved one transcends all notions of time. The ache, the longing, lives in the very essence of our human nature.

03

Grief is an enigmatic path; Grief isn't linear.—

If we were to create a line graph of our grief journeys, it would be surprising for scientists to discover no discernible pattern.

Within the ebb and flow of our grief, we encounter good and bad days interwoven in a twisted dance.

Embracing this is how we move with our grief. Labeling and attempting to confine it only breeds resistance. Progress lies *not* in imposing a specific timeline but in surrendering to the ever-changing flow of our grief and learning to move on with acceptance and dignity.

Grief is evidence of love lost.

It serves as a poignant symbol of our love, our desire to cherish and remember those individuals and relationships that hold deep significance in our lives.

It's instinctively human: both beautiful and painful. By labeling grief as a problem in this sacred space, By labeling grief as a problem to solve, we carry it. By leaning into our pain, we *move with* it.

Grief looms of isolation. Support becomes our lifeline.

Grief defies measurement, transcending the confines of milestones as the 5 Stages of Grief imply. It is an ever-evolving journey, an ongoing experience. Pathologizing and diagnosing grief makes it feel abnormal. In reality, it represents so much of the human experience.

Diagnoses can empower us by illuminating how our minds or bodies function differently and offering solutions. However, diagnosing grief only deepens the shame, loneliness, and isolation. No one should feel wrong for grieving beyond a specific date.

We need grief support, not grief diagnosis. By creating space for its expression, allowing its capacity to unfold without restraint.

Unlock the Profound Power of Healing with EMBRACE
The 7 Stages of Grief Alignment

Are you prepared to immerse yourself on a journey of healing and self-discovery?

Step into a sphere of authenticity, truth, and love as you immerse yourself in the unparalleled wisdom and guidance offered in the transformative EMBRACE course. This course goes beyond the ordinary, offering a depth of healing that will leave an indelible impact.

What sets EMBRACE apart? It emerges from the heart of an expert grief practitioner, infused with the spirit of authenticity and infused by a genuine desire to empower and support individuals on their unique healing journeys.

EMBRACE offers a transformative approach that transcends traditional teachings.

Through this meticulously crafted course, you will unlock the tools and techniques to navigate the depths of grief, embracing healing and growth. The 7 Stages of Grief Alignment workbook becomes your trusted companion, providing compassionate guidance through each stage. It empowers you to honor your journey, embrace your emotions, and pave the way for a purposeful shift.

However, EMBRACE's path forward still needs to be completed. Those interested in learning more and becoming certified "Healing it Forward" practitioners will find that this course provides a beautiful opportunity to do just that. As a trained professional, you will be honored to assist others on their journey to wholeness and personal development.

The EMBRACE program is an astonishing journey of self-discovery and empowerment, not simply another healing class. It encourages you to look within, where you'll find the key to your inner wisdom and the key to your recovery. Along the journey, you'll be surrounded and transformed by a community of like-minded spirits who share your unyielding dedication to growth and give support and encouragement.

Are you prepared to take your life's most incredible life-changing healing journey? Join us on this life-altering adventure, where our north stars are sincerity, honesty, and love. Learn the true meaning of pivoting with intent through your experience with EMBRACE. Your healing journey awaits, and we are here to walk alongside you every step of the way.

Are You Ready?

ALL RIGHT, GRIEF WARRIORS:

We're breaking up with the 5 Stages of Grief

Meet your new boo,
the 7 Stages of Grief Alignment!

The 7 Stages of Grief Alignment knows no order. They are not
steps but continual pillars, symbols, and actions to make
space for grief in your growth.

*Words hold immense power, and we choose to
transform our grief rather than diagnose it.*

The Grief Warrior

EMBRACE

THE 7 STAGES OF GRIEF ALIGNMENT

01

EXPRESS
Let your emotions guide you and experience the joy and fulfillment of expressing your true self through journaling and artistic exploration.

02

MEDITATE
Embrace the power of sitting with your grief, opening your heart, and leaning into the serenity of the present moment, creating space for healing and growth.

03

BE PRESENT
Pause. Observe and relinquish the need for constant busyness, and tune into the depths of your feelings. Embrace the beauty, opportunity, and purpose in this moment.

04

REJUVENATE
Reignite your zest for life, nourish your soul, and elevate your vibrations through the transformative power of self-care. Rediscover what it means to feel truly alive.

05

AWAKEN
Awaken the part of you that's been hiding. Reclaiming lost joy, energy, and vibrance. Rediscover the essence of your true self, waiting to be revealed.

06

CONNECT
Grief can separate us from true ourselves, making us feel like trapped observers of our lives. Reconnect physically, mentally, and spiritually to find your center and regain a sense of control and profound connection.

07

EAT HEALTHY
Nourish your body with the fuel it craves for strength and vitality. Embrace the sensory delight of flavors, textures, and intuitive connection as your body receives each healthy bite.

What 'stage' speaks to you?

IF YOU'RE READY TO TURN YOUR PAIN INTO FUEL...

Your past can lead you to your purpose.

Your pain can become your fuel to embody and fulfill that purpose. It's time to heal the resilient spirit within you, the one who has overcome more than imagined possible.

Unclench your jaw. Let out a sigh of relief - and stop running. We can't change our pasts. e may not alter our pasts, but we can find peace in our history and shape our futures by nurturing our souls in the present moment.

Each of us possesses a unique narrative shaped by our experiences. While we may not always have control over the plot, we have the power to choose the underlying theme. Let us craft our stories around the essence of healing rather than being defined by pain.

Rise as a warrior, not just a survivor. I am here to guide you because I believe in your strength.

It's time to take hold of the reins and chart a path toward healing, love, and inner strength.

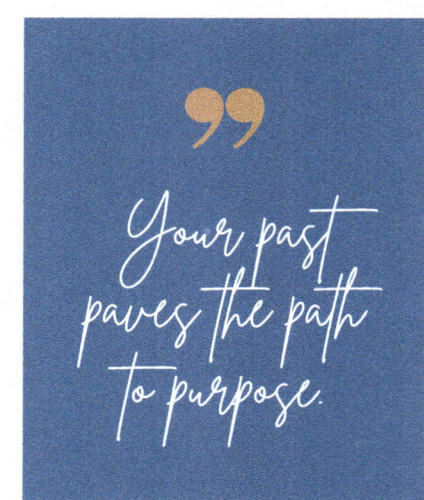

Your past paves the path to purpose.

i believe in you.

Grab a pen, and we'll embark on your new journey together.

PIVOT *with* PURPOSE

My vocation is a sacred calling, where every word, line, and page is carefully crafted with intention and purpose. My vocation extends far beyond the conventional realms. It transcends the boundaries of traditional academia and ventures into the realm of energy and transcendence.

Having traversed the depths of deep trauma and loss, I intimately understand the weight of grief and despair. Yet, I alchemize that suffering into meaning through the art of writing, creating, and teaching. I am fueled by authentic and intentional love in every breath of my life.

It is not a love born out of obligation but a love that empowers and inspires, beckoning others to rise above their fears and embrace the limitless possibilities that lie within them.

To me, this is the very essence of sacredness.

Let this inspire you that, no matter your challenges, you can *Pivot with Purpose* and manifest life in alignment with your highest energy. As your Grief Warrior® mentor, I will guide you on a sacred transformation journey.

I HAD TWO CHOICES:
Retreat Or Renew

When my first-born son passed away, grief consumed me. I could have withdrawn from life, but a fire within me refused to give up. It was then that I realized grief is the expression of love. It's our mind and heart's way of grappling with loss. It requires embracing the unknown, for life itself is unpredictable, regardless of our beliefs.

In rediscovering the magic of life, I rekindled my commitment to live truly. The grief didn't vanish, but it became more manageable. I started noticing the small things that bring joy to life. Each day became an adventure filled with endless possibilities. With an open heart, I welcomed the uncertainties that came my way. While the aftermath of a loss can leave us feeling hopeless, the strength to persevere can lead to unexpected achievements. Withdrawing may seem tempting, but it only perpetuates a downward spiral. We can move forward and rediscover joy by renewing our commitment to purposeful living.

I crafted the 7 Stages of Grief Alignment to renew my commitment—a guide from eleven years of personal experience and introspection. My book, A Son's Gift, became a testament to living intentionally after unforeseen circumstances. This challenge navigates the unexpected tragedies that may befall us, particularly if we face intense grief for the first time. Each stage holds significance, and we must traverse them daily. It isn't always easy, but a life infused with meaning and purpose is worthwhile.

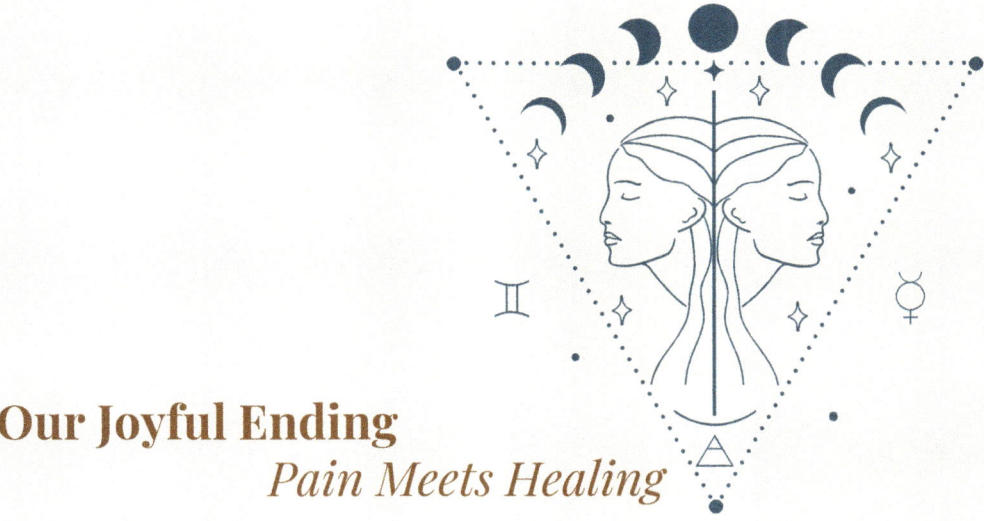

Our Joyful Ending
Pain Meets Healing

Once upon a time,

...in the whimsical land of Serenityville, a group of courageous warriors known as the Serene Seekers set forth on a remarkable quest—the Journey of Healing it Forward. Guided by the wise and enchanting fairy Seraphina, they discovered the secret power of acceptance. The goal was to align with the 7 Stages of Grief and release the mystical power inside.

The Serene Seekers set out on their journey full of bravery and love. As they wandered through enchanted forests and sparkling waterways, they experienced times of hardship. They didn't shy away since they knew the answer to their problems resided within themselves.

The Serene Seekers blazed a trail based on the ancient wisdom of the 7 Stages of Grief Alignment. Each phase—"Express," "Meditate," "Be Present," "Rejuvenate," "Awaken," "Connect," and "Eat Healthy"—held a vital piece of the puzzle to their recovery and development.

Under Seraphina's guidance, the Serene Seekers learned that pain was not their enemy but a teacher to be embraced. It became a part of their story, a testament to their courage and resilience. United in their journey, they supported one another, sharing stories and offering solace when needed. Their empathy and compassion wove a love web across Serenityville.

By embracing their pain, the Serene Seekers discovered the profound magic of healing it forward. They realized their healing could inspire and uplift others, spreading hope and resilience far and wide.

The Serene Seekers' journey through the 7 Stages of Grief Alignment showcased the power of acceptance and showed the world how beautiful it can be. Their travels exemplified the concept of "healing it forward," the idea that one person's kindness may positively impact others.

And so, the Serene Seekers continued their noble quest, fueled by determination and love. Together, they embarked on the Journey of Healing It Forward, embracing their pain, sharing their stories, and spreading seeds of healing throughout Serenityville and beyond.

This uplifting tale illustrates the power of facing our suffering and moving with "Healing it Forward."

HOW TO
Sit *with* Your Grief

ACKNOWLEDGE IT.

OWN IT.

EXPLORE IT.

THERE ARE 3 FUNDAMENTAL
STEPS TO EMBRACING YOUR GRIEF

FEEL *and* ACKNOWLEDGE IT

Feel - Dive into the Depths of Emotion In the first step. We will learn the art of feeling. Relax your body and mind by closing your eyes and taking a few slow, deep breaths. Don't oppose or judge the feelings you're experiencing.

Are you on the verge of purging, overwhelmed by a storm of pain, guilt, shame, betrayal, or envy?

In EMBRACE, you will understand the depth of your pain through emotional exploration. Embracing our feelings shows respect for the integrity of our experience and lays the foundation for healing.

To *acknowledge* is to embrace the power of acceptance with the courage to feel. It is easy to dismiss our grief, burying it beneath layers of denial or self-judgment. But this step teaches us to embrace our pain by acknowledging its presence. Let go of the urge to push your feelings aside or berate yourself for struggling. Instead, recognize that grief is a natural and valid experience. When you own your suffering, you allow yourself the time and perspective to determine what's causing it.

OWN YOUR FEELINGS
of Pain, Grieving, Loss

Understanding your feelings is the first step, but owning your pain is crucial. Grief is often associated with a side of ourselves that we prefer to ignore, so we dismiss it. However, pushing your emotions aside or criticizing yourself for struggling can worsen things. Instead, it's essential to accept your pain as a natural and valid experience and take responsibility for it.

By holding yourself accountable, you can create the space and understanding necessary to delve deeper into the issue and uncover its root cause. This process of self-exploration allows you to work with your pain rather than fighting against it, leading to gradual healing and release from its grasp. With time, you may find that your pain becomes a source of wisdom and inspiration, helping you cultivate self-compassion, acceptance, and strength.

So, don't dismiss your pain or judge yourself for feeling it. Embrace it as an opportunity for self-discovery and growth, and let it guide you on your journey.

ARE YOU LIVING A LIFE *of Denial*?

Denial is a tempting refuge, an escape from facing the truth that awaits us. But is it truly living?

Yet, in denying our true selves, we rob life of its vibrant colors. We become sleepwalkers, traversing existence without truly seeing or experiencing its wonders. Disconnected from our emotions, we numb ourselves to the essence of our being, avoiding the aspects of life we dare not confront.

Grief has a way of leaving us feeling empty, disconnected from the world. Faced with such turbulent emotions, it is crucial to remain present. Opening ourselves to the surrounding reality allows us to reestablish our connection to ourselves and the world surrounding us.

If denial has become your shield for too long, it is time to confront the truth. Though it may be a painful pilgrimage, evading your emotions and sidestepping the obstacles that impede your growth will only perpetuate your suffering. To live a life of integrity and authenticity, we must be brave enough to acknowledge our wounds and fears.

Embrace the journey, for it may come with its share of challenges. Remember, transformation is not an overnight process; it requires time and intense dedication. But as you courageously confront your pain, you will uncover hidden wells of strength within. Say goodbye to denial and welcome the truth of your existence. With each intentional step, you carve a path toward a life filled with authenticity and purpose.

The path ahead may be arduous, but you are not alone. I am here to offer my unwavering support, accompanying you through every stride of this transformative journey. Embrace your inner resilience and have faith in the healing process.

Trust yourself and step boldly into a life of authenticity and growth. You have the power to rewrite your story.

The Guiding Light of *Embrace* Nurturing Those in Grief

Faced with another's grief, we often find ourselves at a loss for words. The profound pain and sorrow they bear can leave us powerless, uncertain of how to offer solace in their darkest hours. Yet, amidst the vastness of this challenge, there exists a flare of hope—a well-crafted grief book, EMBRACE.

In these pages, you'll find a companion journal that will bring comfort and understanding to those roaming the twisted path of sorrow.

While it is impossible to erase the pain, EMBRACE can soothe the aching heart and guide one's steps through the obstacles of grief.

The sentimental narratives make the emotions' kaleidoscope more explicit and the burden of grief more tolerable. As a treasured tool in your grief bag, the 7 Stages of Grief Alignment provides a roadmap for the griever and their companions, fostering awareness and healing.

Yet, it is crucial to remember that when supporting someone living in grief, the gift of your presence and enduring willingness to listen outweighs any words of wisdom or reassurance.

With its intricate nuances, grief often leaves those who mourn feeling isolated and misunderstood. EMBRACE is a heartfelt promise that assures you that you are not alone in your journey.

EMBRACE will offer hope and encouragement, reminding readers they are not alone in their sorrow. Consider giving them a copy to support a friend or loved one during grief.

If you want to support a friend or loved one during grief, consider giving them a copy of EMBRACE! You want the support of your loved ones, and the same goes for them needing you. As with any journey in life, the journey of grief as a team, we got this!

The Healing Dance of Grief
Nurturing the Spirit *within*

When someone close to us dies tragically, we are engulfed by an overwhelming sense of loss, accompanied by a symphony of painful emotions. We journey through this dimension of grief, uniquely navigating its twists and turns. Some shed tears like raindrops from a stormy sky, others ignite with fiery anger, while some retreat into the solitude of their inner world. These reactions, these expressions of grief, are the rivers that flow from the depths of our souls. We must honor them, for within these expressions lie the seeds of self-awareness and the catalysts for healing.

It's simple to feel disoriented and overwhelmed in today's fast-paced, ever-evolving society. The grieving process is a multifaceted test; we all long for the loving company of a compassionate that requires us to seek comfort from those who can relate. As a holistic practitioner, I stand ready with the tools and resources to accompany you on this sacred pilgrimage. Drawing upon my extensive experience, I offer a sanctuary where your voice can be heard, your story shared, and your healing ignited.

Discerning the way forward is exhausting in life's chaotic orchestra, where confusion and uncertainty reign. The weight of emotional pain may tempt us to forge ahead, mindlessly seeking an escape from the obstacles that hinder our progress. Yet, dear soul, a profound wellspring of resilience and strength lies within you. Developing spiritual growth can lead to a limitless abundance of peace and stability. Nurturing your connection with a higher power or the wisdom within you can help you navigate life's most brutal storms with grace and serenity. As you enter this sacred journey of spiritual expansion, you will uncover newfound capacities to navigate life's turbulent seas, supporting your passage and extending a loving hand to those who traverse similar paths.

The road may appear dimly lit as you tread its winding path. Yet, within you resides a radiance of faith, highlighting the darkness for those who desire comfort in your presence. Even when grief looms, keep hope alive in the sanctuary of your heart. I encourage optimism even in the darkness. Envision a shining star, your inner strength shining its light into the deepest crevices of despair. As you gaze upon the darkness, challenge fear and vulnerability to manifest and transform into a conduit for healing. By embracing the full spectrum of your being, shadows, and all, you control the destiny of self-empowerment. Even in the trenches of darkness, your intense light inspires and uplifts those who witness your strength and courage.

Remember that you are never alone in the sacred dance of grief, where each step is steeped with the essence of unconditional love. Reach out, Warrior, to those who can guide and support you on this transformative pilgrimage. Together, you will honor the pain, nurture your spirit, and spin a tapestry of healing that extends far beyond the realms of grief. Let the rhythm of your heart guide you, as it holds within it the tune of perseverance, the harmony of optimism, and the assurance of rejuvenation.

Shadows become tools that help shape
Who You Are...

The Symphony of *Empathy* Navigating Responses to *Grief*

Why do some people run when I embrace my sadness?

Have you ever felt alone in your sadness because others choose to ignore or withdraw from you?

It's disheartening to question whether you deserve support or understanding. It can be challenging for those not accustomed to dealing with intense emotions like grief to face their feelings. Fear, unfamiliarity, and a lack of knowledge about responding supportively could all contribute to their feelings.

It can feel like others are trying to hide from the truth of your experience and being when they avoid hearing about your sorrowful tale. It might make you feel invisible, alone, and desperate for approval. An essential part of the grieving process is vulnerability, which searches for comfort in human connection and comprehension.

However, it is essential to note that only some can face and hold space for strong emotions, especially if they have not experienced something comparable. Their insecurity stems from a need for more ease with showing emotion. It's important not to take their reaction personally; instead, give yourself time and space to work through your feelings.

Be gentle with yourself and embrace the understanding that not everyone will comprehend or offer enduring support on this path. With time, you'll meet people who can hold the sacred space for your grief, opening doors to vital life lessons and opportunities for new relationships.

There can be many reasons why people don't respond to your melancholy expressions. Some people may struggle with displays of intense emotion, while others may feel ill-equipped to respond to someone who is deeply sorrowful. In certain instances, people may even fear that witnessing your sadness will awaken their dormant pain. It is essential to acknowledge that each person uniquely navigates grief, and adverse reactions to your sorrow do not show a lack of care or concern. Give them breathing room to deal with their feelings; they may discover the strength to help you.

As you continue your grief journey, remember that your emotions are valid and that your need for support is real. Seek solace in those who can hold space for your grief, and let go of the notion that everyone will understand. The dance of empathy requires patience and calls for self-compassion. If you care for yourself during this process, you show others how accepting melancholy can strengthen the spirit.

The Whispers of *Compassion*
Nurturing *Empathy* Through Small Acts

Empathy's complex webs of connection strengthen relationships during the grieving process. A kind touch, reassuring words, and a listening ear can go a long way toward alleviating emotional pain. During sadness, expressions of sympathy transform into a beautiful melody of support, kindness, and concern.

Even the tiniest gestures can convey the magnitude of affection and concern in moments of quiet reflection. Sincerity and love injected into the most straightforward actions can illuminate the darkest places. These seemingly insignificant acts go beyond words to bring solace to the soul. By doing these nice things for them, we can let them know they have our undying support and are not alone.

Sometimes, the answer lies not in words but in the silent embrace of companionship. To stand beside someone in their darkest hours to honor their wishes can transcend an act of compassion. You become a sanctuary of support for their wounded soul. Becoming a lifeline amidst the chaos by offering practical help, running errands, and preparing nourishing meals demonstrates that our warmth extends beyond mere words to sacred stillness.

They provide a sympathetic ear that accepts their suffering without judgment or making demands. We become instruments of compassion and wisdom, holding the door open for their recovery.

When words fail, being there and knowing how grateful we are can help comfort a broken spirit. Therefore, let us recognize the significance of greeting cards, reassuring embraces, and quiet moments of reflection. Aim to personify empathy, compassion, and concern. We become the vessels through which comfort is delivered, mending the broken parts of a mourning person's spirit in those quiet times.

You can use the following phrases:

My heart goes out to you; I'm sorry this is happening to you.
"What is your loved one's name?"
"What do you say we get some lunch together? Please tell me more about (insert name of cherished one here)."

The Unseen Language of Sorrow
Embracing *Understanding* and *Letting Go*

It's frustrating when those close to you don't understand how much your loss means to you. Some wonder if avoiding those who can't share our sorrow is right. But let's PAUSE to think about this:

No matter how well you articulate your pain, not everyone can comprehend complex emotions. Despite our efforts to articulate our pain, some may struggle to grasp its true essence. In these situations, letting go of our dependence on their comprehension is not a sign of a lack of strength or inability. Our efforts to help them understand the inexplicable would be well-spent.

Don't you think it's wonderful to imagine a world where empathy is cultivated and understanding becomes a part of our collective etiquette? While that ideal may be far off, we can take comfort in the company of those who share our values and offer proper understanding and support. Seek comfort in knowing you are not alone on your grief journey. By doing so, we create space for our healing, allowing our sorrow to unfold in its way, guided by our resilience and the support of those who truly understand.

01

Let us find comfort in the arms of those who truly understand and share our pain on this developing path of sorrow. Even if others can't understand our pain, it's reassuring that some would listen with empathy and provide a safe place to heal.

02

In the depths of sorrow, we are faced with a "griefosophical" lesson:

We are the chosen ones entrusted with the sacred duty of carrying the unseen language of sorrow. It is not a burden to bear but a calling that sets us apart from others. Our connection with our departed loved one runs deep, transcending the comprehension of others. The love we shared with them was unique, profound, and intimate, coloring our grief in hues that may mystify those who did not experience the same depth of connection.

Rather than harboring resentment or seeking understanding from those who cannot offer it, we can shift our perspective. It helps to think of ourselves as spiritual vessels that have solemnly promised to bear the burden of our grief. To mourn together is to witness the strength of love and reveal the depth of our connection.

By letting go of the expectation that everyone will understand our grief, we unlock a sense of communal understanding only discernible by our innermost beings. We become a collective source of higher consciousness. Our common grief language helps us bond with those who resonate with our vibe.

So, Warriors, Let up, hoping other people share your pain with you. Embrace the idea that you are connected to a group of people who "get it," and you become a force that cannot be stopped together. Make use of your suffering as a starting point for introspection and growth.

In doing so, you give tribute to the unconditional love you shared with your departed loved one and become that twinkle who walks this path of grief.

In grief, we are chosen to carry
the unseen language of sorrow,
a testament to our love and
resilience.

Unveiling the Art of
Respecting *Grief*

In this era of digital connectivity, we find ourselves conditioned to swiftly move on and brush aside the depths of our grief. Glossing over the importance of grieving and grief acceptance might be easy in today's fast-paced world. However, grief encompasses far more than prolonged sadness; it is an emotional journey that demands time, reverence, empathy, and patience to mend.

Loss, especially the irreparable loss of love, is at the heart of mourning. When we suffer a profound loss, it changes who we are and shines a light on what gives our lives true purpose. The path to recovery and growth lies in sincerely accepting our suffering.

Nobody enjoys being hurt, and most people will try to avoid it. However, suffering is a part of being human and must be faced head-on. Grief and loss, and the emotional sorrow they cause, are experiences all humans share at some point. Neither can we expect anybody else to take away our suffering, but we can show compassion, which can teach us a great deal about how to deal with the misery of others. Through compassion, we see that the suffering of others is natural and merits our whole attention.

The ability to empathize with others serves as a helpful reminder that there is no single "correct" way to deal with suffering. It is unnecessary to have all the solutions to be compassionate; all we need to do is be there for people when they are suffering.

So, when we see a loved one going through a tough time, let's not rush to ease their suffering. Instead, let's give our undivided attention to becoming wise. By doing so, we show them the kindness and consideration they deserve. There is an act of tremendous bravery, tenacity, and grit at the heart of mourning, an act that teaches profound truths about what it is to be human. So, let's not rush past the remembrances of limitless, unconditional LOVE.

Embracing the *Everlasting* **Journey**

BOTTOM *line*

One of life's greatest challenges is coming to terms with the fact that mourning is never really "done." We may reach a point where the raw pain of our loss has begun to fade, but the scars remain. These scars can be a source of strength and comfort. They remind us of the loved ones we have lost and help us appreciate life's fragility.

But keep in mind that you will never fully "get over" your loss. It is an ongoing journey that we all must travel. There may be days when the path is smooth and the going is rough. But eventually, we will reach our destination: a place where we can find peace and happiness again.

Healing is an ever-unfolding journey, an intricate dance of self-discovery and growth. As we set out on our journey, we recognize that our wounds are not who we are but a testament to our capacity to love fiercely and persevere through adversity. Unconditional self-love feeds the soul and opens the door to healing on all levels. Putting aside baggage and focusing on what brings us joy might help us find inner freedom.

You may find that your relationship with your loved one changes as you move through grief. Their presence becomes a source of strength and comfort, reminding you of their eternal love. You gradually rebuild your life as you heal, carrying their memory within you. Their spirit entwines with yours, illuminating the path to a meaningful existence.

While healing may never be complete, grief can propel you toward a more positive emotional journey. Embracing and expressing your grief healthily allows for soul healing to begin.

express

meditate

be present

rejuvenate

awaken

connect

eat healthy

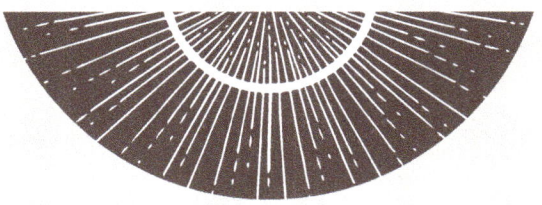

DOES EMBRACE
Speak to You?

Explore the transformative power of The 7 Stages of GRIEF Alignment workbook journal, designed to support you authentically and effectively on your grief journey. Each stage of this journal is carefully crafted to nurture your physical and mental well-being, empowering you to strengthen critical aspects of your health as you navigate through the aftermath of a traumatic event. Embracing these stages will lead you to greater strength, resilience, and a revitalized sense of purpose.

Drawing from personal experiences of loss and trauma, I created the 7 Stages of GRIEF Alignment mini journal to assist those willing to EMBRACE in their healing process. Within its pages, you'll discover practices that have deeply impacted my grief journey, enabling me to navigate through the pain and embrace genuine growth mindfully. These practices have brought about timeless healing, from releasing old attachments to rebuilding a lost sense of unconditional love.

This eternal healing perfectly captures the beauty of "Healing."

Whether at the beginning of your grief journey or making progress, embracing the stages outlined in this journal can ease the burden and infuse joy into your life. Let's say you've had enough and are ready to start living again. Please join me on the 7 Stages of the GRIEF Alignment workbook journal's transformational journey, or go even further and earn your Certified Wellness Warrior designation.

Take a deep breath, stay resilient, and remember that even in the darkest moments, we possess the inner strength to move forward. Embrace this opportunity and witness its profound impact on your life. Not doing so would be a mistake.

EXPRESS

Welcome to the First Stage of Grief Alignment: Express. In this stage, we encourage you to unleash your thoughts, feelings, and trauma through emotional journaling. By embracing this practice, you voice your emotions and release anxiety, triggers, and pain.

Reflect on its meaning in your grief journey and explore its significance. Use your notebook as a place of refuge where you may explore who you are and how you got here. Allow your own words to heal and shape your spirit.

Three ways you can integrate 'Express' into your daily therapy:

Emotional Journaling
Write freely each day to express and process your emotions.

Artistic Expression
Engage in creative activities to communicate and release emotions.

Verbal Communication
Share your feelings with a trusted person or practitioner for support and validation.

Expression is the key to unlocking our connection, allowing us to co-create a reality rooted in love and acceptance. So say their name, share your story, feel every moment, and remember—you are here for a reason. And always remember—you are here with a purpose. You have the power to create. So keep expressing yourself—you have everything it takes to thrive!

How will you express today?

MEDITATE

Have you ever explored the richness of meditation? It offers a gateway to discovering tranquility and clarity in grief or challenging moments. By dedicating time to cultivating mindful awareness, we unlock the potential for remarkable revelations.
With each intentional inhalation and exhalation, we create a sacred space within ourselves, allowing us to confront our emotions from a higher perspective.

Discover peace in nature's embrace, where meditation unveils transformative insights.

Pause for a moment and ask yourself: When was the last time you truly paused and immersed yourself in the vivid reality of "here"? It is in the here and now, the ever-present moment, where true existence lives. It is within this moment that the miracle of life unfolds.

BE PRESENT

'Be Present' is the 3rd Stage of Grief Alignment, encouraging us to be still. Society often expects us to conform to specific standards, but we have the power to within ourselves begin a path toward wellness simply by showing up.

Being present allows us to reconnect with life, love, and feel again.

Let's focus on being present and mindful. Pay attention to your breath - feel the rise and fall of your chest and let it move like a symphony's crescendo. Focus on the present and feel the caress of each inhale and exhale. Take in the vibrant feelings that sweep your entire being, and let them merge with the present moment.

Allowing your emotions to take over can be liberating. Accepting and working with our feelings without hesitation or judgment is crucial. Whatever those emotions may be, it's okay to feel them. Take a moment to permit yourself to step back, allowing your soul to have time within this very breath.

REJUVENATE

For true revitalization, we must turn inward and examine our bodily, mental, and spiritual states.

It can help us reclaim our vitality and lead us toward joy and fulfillment, especially when dealing with the loss of a loved one or the constant stresses of modern life. Transformation comes with self-reflection, inner growth, and healing. You have the power to do this!

By embracing new challenges and striving to grow in every aspect of our lives, we can reignite the spark and fire up our souls. So, why wait? We can rejuvenate and awaken joy at every level with determination and self-acceptance.

Reflecting on our loved ones and the gifts they gave us can also help rejuvenate our lives in their honor. Whether remembering a favorite memory or reaching out to those who supported us during difficult times, each act deepens the connection between us and our loved ones, even as they move beyond the physical world.

Ultimately, we choose how to react to grief, but by acknowledging our journey and embracing joy, we can find strength in our spirit again.

AWAKEN

In the 5th Stage of Grief Alignment, Awaken, you are invited to embrace the essence of being fully alive and anchored in the present moment. Retaining and shielding ourselves from raw emotions and harsh realities is expected in the depths of grief.

Awakening is the key that unlocks the door to our inner resilience and rekindles our faith in the truth that lies before us.

Pause and contemplate your life as it stands today. Allow this fresh perspective to offer a broader view, enabling you to observe your journey from a distance. In this introspection, you may realize that all you need lives within, and a vast expanse of possibilities awaits you on the horizon.

Let's embrace the awakening, as it acts as a catalyst that propels us forward with a renewed sense of vitality and purpose on our journey.

CONNECT

In the 'C' of EMBRACE, we find the power of connection in the 6th Stage of Grief. As we make our way through the complexities of this world, now is the moment to strengthen our connection to ourselves, our spirit, and our mind. While it may pose challenges, remember that we all thrive on daily connections.

How will you choose to CONNECT today?

Your mind. Your body. Your spirit.

Make a conscious effort to connect with yourself by dedicating just five minutes to express gratitude, a walk in nature, engaging in reflective journaling, cooking, creating, or allowing yourself to be still. Focus on self-care and self-reflection to enhance your well-being.

Tune in to your needs and honor them, for it is in these connections that true healing and growth can flourish.

EAT HEALTHY

In the final stage of our grief alignment journey, we are called to embrace the importance of nourishing ourselves through healthy eating. As we have journeyed through the different stages of grief in our course, we have learned the significance of addressing our emotional, mental, and spiritual needs. Now, we focus on the physical aspect of our well-being, recognizing that what we put into our bodies directly impacts our healing process.

Eating healthy becomes the inner thread that weaves all the stages of our grief alignment journey. By nourishing ourselves with wholesome, nutrient-rich foods, we provide our bodies with the fuel to support our healing from the inside out. We actively participate in our healing process by prioritizing foods promoting strength, vitality, and well-being.

As we continue our journey beyond grief, let us carry healthy eating lessons. Let us embrace the power of wholesome foods to support our ongoing healing and growth.

It is through this holistic approach that we can truly thrive and create a life that is vibrant, nourished, and filled with joy.

YOUR INNER
spiritual warrior!

EMBRACE is the ultimate exhilarating journey of healing and transformation. This course is not just a certification—it is a profound commitment to healing and a powerful dedication to moving forward with purpose.

We encounter countless challenges that test our resilience and tempt us to give up. Yet, deep within us lies an untapped well of strength, waiting patiently to be discovered and unleashed. This course empowers you to tap into that inner strength, unlock your full potential, and become the vessel to *healing it forward*.

The key lies in listening to your heart and trusting your instincts. By tuning into the untapped wisdom at the core of your being, you gain the clarity and guidance needed to navigate any obstacle that comes your way. With a resilient focus, you cultivate the courage and determination required to **move with** emotional barriers.

As you EMBRACE this journey, you discover that nurturing your inner world positively impacts your external world, cultivating meaningful connections with others, and investing in your self-enlightenment. The key lies in listening to your heart and trusting your instincts.

The 7 Stages of Grief Alignment will be your guiding light as you EMBRACE each stage of grief in your own time. Recognize that these stages are not linear processes; you may move back and forth between them as you navigate your unique grief journey. This flexibility allows you to honor your experience and progress at your own pace.

Are you ready to step into your power as a Certified Grief Wellness Coach?
Sign up today and trust your inner calling, take that leap of faith, and let your guiding light illuminate the path of healing and transformation for yourself and others.

A Graceful Pivot to Purpose

you've made it

You are now ready to **EMBRACE** our Third Stage:

— be present —

That's the blessing and power of **pivoting with purpose.**

What are the 7 Stages of Grief Alignment?
Express. **M**editate.
Be Present. **R**ejuvenate.
Awaken. **C**onnect. **E**at Healthy.

Healing begins with acceptance and alignment transforms us through embracing our life's experiences.

**The empower of embracing is in your next chapter –
are you ready to turn the page?**

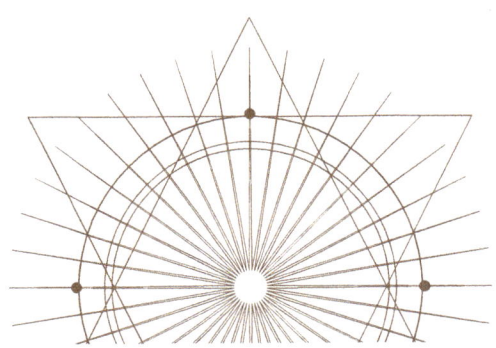

Table of Contents

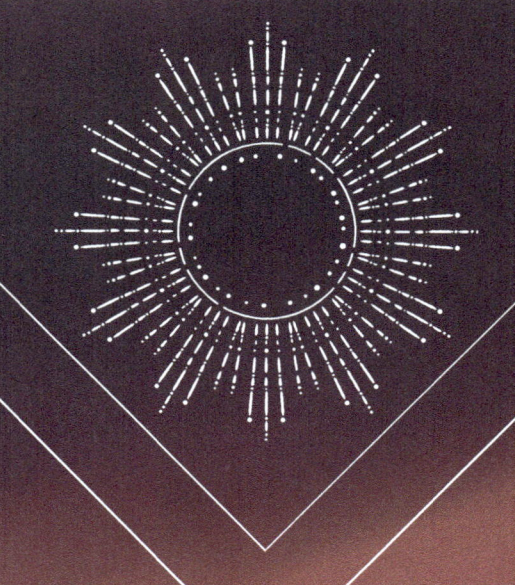

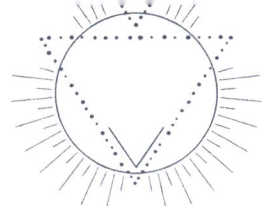

Finding Presence *with* Grief

A note of love

Transforming Grief into Growth: Navigating the Journey with Resilience and Purpose

Grief is an inevitable part of life's journey, and while experiencing pain may be unavoidable, it doesn't have to be without purpose. Everyone's experience is unique, and it can be challenging to remember this when all we have in common is suffering.

By engaging with our emotions and staying present in the moment, we can begin to make meaningful connections between pain and growth. This unlocks new levels of resilience and helps us find direction and renewed love for life.

Incorporating Solitude for Self-Reflection

The journey through grief can be long and arduous, but it is possible to emerge on the other side feeling healed. One often overlooked component of this journey is solitude. Taking time alone can provide valuable insight into our emotions, helping us navigate difficult waters toward peace and self-connection.

Embracing the Power of Being Human

Finding our inner strength during grief requires us to embrace the power of being human. It is essential to allow ourselves a safe place to cry and process our emotions honestly and authentically rather than masking them with false joy.

Balancing Solitude and Support

While being with loved ones during isolation can bring comfort, solitude can allow us to process our emotions without fear or judgment. To heal from grief effectively, we must listen intently to ourselves, finding the perfect balance between our need for solitude and the comforting embrace of others. Seeking support when necessary is also crucial for a balanced recovery.

By embracing our emotions, allowing ourselves room for self-expression, and finding balance in solitude and support, we can transform grief into growth, emerging from the journey with newfound resilience and purpose.

Journal Prompts

Take some time to think about how grief can play a role in your journey. Is there a way to find meaning and personal growth through the experience of pain and loss?

_____
_____
_____
_____
_____
_____
_____
_____

Explore the balance between embracing your emotions and connecting to the present moment. How can you build a connection between your grief and personal resilience, allowing for new directions and love in your life?

_____
_____
_____
_____
_____
_____
_____
_____

Consider the role of solitude in your grief journey. How can taking time alone provide insight while seeking support and connection from trusted loved ones? How can you balance solitude and social support for a balanced recovery?

_____
_____
_____
_____
_____
_____

Exercise

For every chapter exercise, locate a peaceful area and focus on being fully present.

Coping with grief can be a challenging process.However, by practicing mindfulness and creating a peaceful environment for yourself, you can find inner calmness and guide yourself through this difficult journey.

- Imagine you've stepped outside of yourself and your experience.

- Take an inward journey and be your best friend, understanding you with love and compassion.

- As this observer, you've just been told it's your responsibility to understand, support, and extend empathy to this person.

- How do you view your grief experience from this higher, outside perspective?

- As this compassionate observer, how do you respond to these experiences? What words of love and wisdom do you share?

Why not speak kind words to yourself? Take a moment to jot them down as though you're penning a letter to your future self in your diary.

It's important to take time each day to relax and find inner peace. Even just a few minutes can make a difference. Focusing on your breath can help you stay present and calm, leading to a better understanding and resolution of your emotions. Consider incorporating mindfulness into your healing routine.

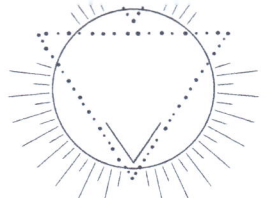

healing your connection

Even though we feel the pain of our losses, grief helps us acknowledge that there was once something unique and valuable in our lives.

A connection still exists with those who have passed on—a supernatural force for healing, hope, and courage to carry forward their legacy.

In my son's situation, his guiding light is ever-present, transcending death by providing opportunities to appreciate beauty and blessings from above.

He led me here to you.

Our connection with our departed loved ones transcends the physical world. Experiences and testimonies from many reveal that death is only a doorway to an existence where we can remain in constant communion. While it may look and feel different, this connection with our loved ones is everlasting, even beyond the veil, if we are open to receiving the messages between the PAUSE.

To tune into this connection, we must find presence. The PAUSE allows us to slow down and accept what is ahead without expectation or judgment; it's time to embrace stillness.

It might lead you to your next great story.

The Release Mantra

"I release all that no longer has a purpose within me. I call in my center of pause and knowing. I ask it to embellish my being with wisdom and dissolve away heavy burdens by releasing and letting go. I ask my inner spirit to trust the process. I understand deeply what you have taught me. I honor every experience with love in my being. The pieces of me are restored." Blessed Be

4

Journal Prompts

Express the unique and valuable aspects of your life that your losses have made you more aware of. How has grief helped you acknowledge the significance of what was once present?

_____
_____
_____
_____
_____
_____
_____
_____
_____

Explore the supernatural force of healing, hope, and courage that comes from maintaining a connection with your departed loved ones. How has this connection provided opportunities to appreciate beauty and blessings?

_____
_____
_____
_____
_____
_____
_____
_____
_____

Share a personal experience or testimony that highlights how your loved one's guiding light continues to influence and lead you. How has their presence transcended death and inspired you to embrace new opportunities and paths?

_____
_____
_____
_____
_____
_____

Exercise

When completing each chapter exercise, it's important to locate a peaceful environment and practice mindfulness.

Finding a quiet space and practicing mindfulness can be helpful in the grieving process.

- Find your way to Pause today. Listen to your inner sanctuary.

- Picture yourself as a ball of white energy. Releasing and Letting Go.

- Maybe it's simply sitting without looking at your phone, watching TV, or responding to the noise. Take a pause, even if it's just for 5 minutes.

- When you are STILL listening to the telepathic waves, write down the messages.

- If you need to, be still in nature. Be still while listening to calming music. However you 'be still' today, know that you are making peace with the present moment and showing yourself and your higher power that you are one step closer to embracing.

Consider the power of finding presence and embracing stillness to tune into the connection with your departed loved ones.

How can you create moments of pause to be open to receiving their messages and guidance?

6

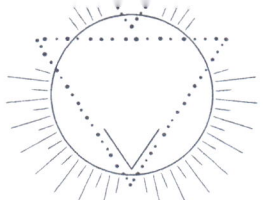

being present in pain

We recognize that simply being present for others can be a powerful way of expressing our support.

I am only here with you right now because of my losses.

What once felt like stumbling blocks became my stepping stones, lifting me to guide and serve others and navigate life after loss.

But even now, I am reminded that forward progress can only come when we embrace our wounds; this allows us to persevere in love.

In finding presence in our pain, we can also find purpose.

Faced with heartbreaking loss, grieving can be an unexpected source of strength and resilience. When we open ourselves to compassion and service—offering kindness and expecting nothing in return—we can connect more deeply with life. This powerful choice allows us to move forward courageously, despite our sorrows.

Let's all take inspiration from those who have overcome adversity. By learning from our struggles, we can discover a greater sense of purpose that will bring peace to ourselves and others on this journey ahead. May we each find blessings along the way!

We can turn our losses into opportunities for growth and connection with others. To begin, we should focus on being kind and supportive of ourselves in the present moment.

Journal Prompts

Reflect on how your losses have shaped your journey and led you to where you are today. How have your stumbling blocks become stepping stones, guiding you to serve others and navigate life after loss?

_____

_____

_____

_____

Explore the significance of embracing your wounds and persevering in love. How has finding presence in your pain allowed you to find purpose and move forward with courage and resilience?

_____

_____

_____

_____

Share a story of when your grief became a source of strength and resilience. How did opening yourself to compassion and service, offering kindness without expecting anything in return, deepen your connection with life?

_____

_____

_____

_____

Consider the transformational power of turning losses into opportunities for growth and connection. How can you practice self-kindness and support in the present moment, allowing yourself to embrace the blessings and possibilities ahead?

_____

_____

_____

_____

Exercise

For each chapter exercise, make it a point to find a peaceful setting and stay focused on the present moment.

Finding a quiet space and practicing mindfulness can be helpful in the grieving process.

Create a Voice Memo on your phone with the exercise below.

- Find a quiet, meditative space to relax in.

- Once you've found a comfortable position, sit or lie down. Close your eyes between reading each exercise step.

- Now, visualize your pain as a light in your body. This light could be in your head, heart, belly, or body.

- When this light becomes trapped within you, it causes discomfort. That's OK. Allow it to be there by sitting with it.

- Now, imagine what happens when you share this light with others ––it becomes much less heavy and painful. It helps others more than you could've ever imagined.

- All these months or years of carrying this light within you feel less painful because you created purpose. You helped others share their light and feel guided by yours.

- When you're ready, open your eyes and write down your thoughts.

Prioritizing Self-Care: Mindful Journaling Exercises for Inner Peace

Did you know that speaking kind and encouraging words to yourself can be incredibly helpful? Take a moment to write them down in your journal as if you're penning a letter to yourself. Incorporating mindfulness into your life demands that you pause and reflect. Try these journal prompts and exercises to help you live in the present and ultimately find inner peace amidst the chaos of everyday life.

embrace to empower

It's our instinct to run away from pain.

It's a habit to avoid what makes us uncomfortable at all costs.

But we can never move forward if we constantly run away from pain! It will only make the pain more painful and the discomfort more challenging.

So, we'll still feel some resistance when we go against our learned nature and approach our pain, loss, and grief with extended arms. We might even feel a bit threatened.

Embracing uncertainty makes us realize our true strength; pushing ourselves out of our comfort zone can be frightening but ultimately leads to greater confidence.

And then we're finally able to rest. We don't have to run, hide, or fear anymore.

We can sit with the pain, empower our inspiration, and grow and develop resilience on the grief journey. The only way is through diligent commitment leading to discernment.

Release the weight of yesterday, as this moment holds boundless potential and promise. When we fully engage with today, we can use it to mend old wounds and gain strength from our aspirations. Even amidst uncertainty, we can find safety by embracing the present moment.

Discover inner peace and happiness by embarking on a journey of self-reflection. Mindfulness, self-awareness, and resilience are essential for achieving a fulfilling life.

Journal Prompts

You were designed to be different on purpose.

Reflect on a time when you instinctively ran away from pain or discomfort. How did this avoidance affect your ability to move forward and find a resolution?

_____

_____

_____

_____

When approaching your pain, loss, and grief head-on, explore the resistance and fear. How can you shift your mindset to see these moments as opportunities for growth and inner strength?

_____

_____

_____

_____

Consider the power of embracing uncertainty and stepping out of your comfort zone. How can you cultivate confidence and resilience by confronting challenging situations and exploring new possibilities?

_____

_____

_____

_____

What transformative lessons have you learned by sitting with your pain and embracing discomfort on your journey of healing and growth?

_____

_____

_____

_____

Exercise

Locating a peaceful area and focusing on being fully present is essential.

Mornings are best - our theta brain is most active in receiving messages.

- Get 1% more comfortable with the uncomfortable today—nothing major, just a tiny way to show strength.

- Maybe you call up a trusted friend and talk about your feelings. Perhaps you journal, create art, and meditate internally on your creative work.

- Create a map destination you would like to travel to in honor of your grief journey.

- Maybe you decide to go on a 1:1 healing retreat. Choose the destination. Check in with me about your location before you commit!

- Routines with intention are important. Dedicate 15 days a month to Eating Healthy. Book a consultation with me to set this up!

Spend time writing in your journal and listing words that strengthen you. Reflect on your blessings and write an encouraging letter telling yourself that it's okay to take a breather and appreciate your accomplishments.

You Got This, Warrior

liberate your heart

What Does Acceptance Mean?

These widely known 5 stages of grief may only *partially* capture the complex and individual nature of our healing journeys.

Denial.
Anger.
Bargaining.
Depression.
And finally, acceptance.

When it comes to coping with loss, we all have our own distinct stories. Sorrow is a profoundly personal experience, and the traditional stages of sorrow may not always reflect this. Viewing your emotional path as a winding road rather than a rigorous series of steps may be more helpful. Remember that you are not required to follow any one path; everyone's sorrow is unique and will guide them toward healing.

Grief is a complicated and intensely personal experience with the potential for five distinct emotions. But these shouldn't limit our journey. - Instead, we should consider an ongoing exploration of grief that doesn't narrow down any emotion as negative or underdeveloped. Here lies the opportunity to embrace each moment without judgment or stigma attached.

Grief can be a powerful adversary, but you are encouraged to welcome it here. Although carrying grief takes strength, shying away from its presence will only delay proper recovery. Give your pain permission to enter and linger awhile so that it may slowly move through you until there is space for healing within the hollows of your heart.

Acknowledge what is hard for you and embrace this moment as a chance for transformation.

It's important to take a break and enjoy the present moment. Don't worry about what you "should" be doing; pay attention to your body's needs. Take the time to care for yourself without criticism and acknowledge how your body feels.

It's Time to Prioritize Your Emotional Well-being

Take a moment to focus on your emotions and give yourself the time and space you need to experience them. Don't suppress your feelings; permit yourself to feel compassionate – every emotion counts!

Embrace honesty and bravery; don't hesitate to express your emotions. Your story is unique and valuable; don't shy away from sharing it with the world. Take a leap of faith, courageously open up about your feelings, and experience the strength of connecting with the present moment.

Journal Prompts

Reflect on a recent small win or accomplishment that brought you joy or a sense of fulfillment. Describe how it made you feel and how it impacted your overall well-being.

_____

_____

_____

_____

_____

_____

_____

_____

Explore moments in your life when you demonstrated self-love and self-respect. What choices or actions did you take to prioritize your mental, physical, or spiritual well-being? How did these choices positively impact your life?

_____

_____

_____

_____

_____

_____

_____

_____

How can you incorporate small acts of self-care and self-love into your daily routine? How can you prioritize and make space for these activities to cultivate a deeper sense of self-compassion and inner liberation?

_____

_____

_____

_____

_____

_____

Exercise

Find a quiet space - Be Present.

Doing things with INTENTION will build awareness in your PAUSE journey.

- Lean into your emotions and live in the now. Care for them.

- Healthily accept your sadness. Perhaps it's writing in a journal, ranting to a trusted friend, listening to melancholy music, or simply crying.

- Lean into your feelings of optimism.

- Allow yourself to be furious if you are feeling angry.

- It's not about letting your emotions drive or control you ––it's about giving them space to come and go in your body so they don't prevent you. Accept to embrace. Embrace release.

Empower Yourself with Self-Affirmations
Incorporate positive self-talk into your daily routine by writing affirmations in your journal.
Pen a letter to yourself that expresses the words you need to hear.
Feel the sense of liberation coursing through your heart as you take each step towards breaking free from the chains that once held you back. Celebrate small victories along the way and honor yourself with unwavering self-love and respect. This is your journey to liberation, where you rise and soar with the boundless freedom that resides within you.

acceptance to embrace

Loving deeply comes at the expense of grief, a heavy load to bear when our loved ones depart from us. I have experienced this - a sense of hollowness that can seem overwhelming during times of sadness.

We do not seek to bury our loved ones' memories with a fast and superficial solution. Instead, this is an opportunity for us to commemorate their absence in a meaningful way that genuinely pays tribute to them and revels in life.

Through its inclusion, authentic acceptance allows us to explore the depths of our common space, modifying and expanding it as we rediscover life.

Grief and purpose can coexist in harmony - a beautiful journey of self-discovery. It's finding your WHY. It's letting our loving guardian angels guide us to a higher purpose. ——just like my son Nicky led me here to you.

Moving beyond grief can be liberating. Embracing loss can open the door to healing and a deeper appreciation of life's joys.

While life will never be the same again, a new route exists. Allow your sorrows, joys, frustrations, and expectations to accompany the ride - it's okay! This journey promises something fresh but allows you to honor what has been lost or changed forever.

Accepting and embracing this moment is the first step toward healing. Accept to embrace. Embrace to liberate.

Journal Prompts

Embrace Your Why

Reflect on a moment when you experienced the weight of grief and hollowness due to the departure of a loved one. How did this sadness impact you, and how did you navigate it?

_____
_____
_____
_____

Explore ways to commemorate the absence of your loved ones in a meaningful and authentic way. How can you create tributes and rituals that honor their memory and bring a sense of celebration to their life?

_____
_____
_____
_____

Consider the coexistence of grief and purpose in your journey. How can you find your "why" and allow the guidance of your loving guardian angels, like your loved one, to lead you toward a higher purpose? How can embracing loss and honoring what has been lost open the door to healing and a deeper appreciation of life's joys?

_____
_____
_____
_____

What is your WHY?

_____
_____
_____
_____

Exercise

Locate a serene environment and remain attentive in the present moment.
Discernment is the root of Your Evolution.

- Find a comfortable position, whether sitting or lying down.

- Once you're ready, think about your life at this very moment. Not the past or future: the NOW. What is happening right now?
- Let the 'good' and 'bad' coexist.

- Now, take a deep breath through your nose and mouth. Think about what you have control over right now.

- Think about what you are willing to accept right now.

- Take three more deep breaths in and out, and think about how this present moment serves and empowers you.

Remind yourself of the words that will make you feel better. Write them down in your journal as if writing a letter to yourself.

Our health is fluid; simply getting by daily brings you closer to premature aging and disease. To have an abundance on your journey, you must WIN every day.

Small victories occur regularly. The decision to nourish your mind, body, and soul regularly shows SELF LOVE & SELF RESPECT.

Allow this to be your RISE meditation.

one moment at a time

The Alchemy of Presence and Gratitude on the Grief Journey

Time can feel like both an enemy and a savior in the labyrinth of grief. The past haunts, the future looms, and the present moment often gets lost in the shuffle. Yet, it's in the "now" that we find our most potent elixir for healing—presence.

Being present isn't about ignoring the pain or glossing over the complexity of emotions. It's about anchoring yourself in the current moment, allowing yourself to feel, breathe, and exist. When triggers arise, as they inevitably will, the practice of presence becomes your sanctuary.

Reflective Prompt:
What's one situation that recently triggered you? How did you react? Reimagine that moment, but anchor yourself in your presence this time. What changes?
Spinning thoughts into gratitude is the next layer of this alchemy. Gratitude in grief may sound paradoxical, but it's not about being thankful for the loss; it's about finding shards of light in the darkness. It's the warm hug from a friend, the comforting words that resonate, the newfound strength you never knew you had.

Reflective Prompt:
Think of a recent moment when you successfully combined presence and gratitude. How did it feel? What impact did it have on your journey?
Remember, the journey through grief is not a sprint but a marathon, and each moment of presence and gratitude is a step forward. Take it one moment at a time.

Journal Prompts

Embrace This Moment

Identify one moment of darkness on your grief journey. Can you find a shard of light within it? What are you grateful for in that moment?

_____

_____

_____

_____

Explore the power of mindfulness in releasing the burden of past regrets and future worries. How can you cultivate peace and healing by focusing on the present moment and letting go of what you cannot control?

_____

_____

_____

_____

Take advantage of the chance that every new day presents.
How can you approach today with intention and claim it as your own? How can you show up fully and make the most of this day?

_____

_____

_____

_____

Consider the idea od of surrendering to the present moment. What does it mean to let go of resistance and accept the circumstances as they are? How can embracing surrender bring peace and empowerment to your journey through grief?

_____

_____

_____

_____

Exercise

Find a quiet space - Be Present.

Observance is the root of Your Elevation.

- Find a comfortable position to sit or lie down comfortably.

- Take five deep breaths through your nose and five deep breaths out through your mouth.

- Now, draw attention to your surroundings. Look for and name five things you can see in your environment in your head.

- Next, draw attention to and name four things you can feel around you. Maybe it's the ground at your feet, the warmth of your shirt, or the texture of the chair or table you're sitting at.

- Now, find two things you can smell. Our smell is one of the most potent emotional senses we have. Draw your awareness to be present with it.

- Lastly, find one thing you can taste. Whether it's mindfully taking a bite of chocolate or feeling the incredible sensation of water in your mouth, be present with your fifth sense.

Capture the beauty of life in your notebook; write it all down as notes or poems for posterity. These morsels of experience might inspire future creative pursuits and provide insight into a memorable period!

Grand Rising Warrior. I want you to rediscover the joy of the present moment.

I know. It's challenging to do that when your mind is elsewhere, whether in the future or the past.

But we discover actual healing joy here at this moment.

Most "negative" emotions are associated with the past or the future; sadness, loss, and rage connect us to the past, but worry, tension, and fear drag us into the future.

These feelings are very normal. We can heal and go forward by embracing them, as you know.

But when these emotions become our 'default mode,' it's challenging to keep going. It becomes increasingly more difficult to find joy today.

So, we're here to embrace this moment and make it our own by using what I call "Moment-ous Occasions."

Moment-ous Occasions are intentional, present-based actions we can design to focus on the here and now.

It's taking a normal moment and turning it into something extraordinary. It accepts your emotions, recognizes your experiences, and embraces your pain.

It's leaning into the here and now and letting it be enough. It's putting on your "near-sighted glasses" and focusing on what is happening right before you.

Allow yourself to be satisfied if you are happy. Allow yourself to be sad if you are sad. There is no sense of shame or guilt here. There are no "shoulds" or "should'ves" in this sentence.

Embrace the feelings, surroundings, and experiences surrounding you today; make them yours.

Dare to share your emotions. Dare to say their name. Share your story.

Journal Prompts

The More You Share The More You Heal

What everyday moments can you turn into "Moment-ous Occasions" to fully embrace the present moment and find joy in the here and now?

_____

_____

_____

_____

How can you cultivate a mindset of acceptance and non-judgment towards your emotions, experiences, and pain, allowing yourself to fully experience and embrace them without shame or guilt?

_____

_____

_____

_____

How can you create a safe and supportive space for yourself to share your emotions, story, and experiences? How can opening up and expressing your truth contribute to healing and growth on this journey?

_____

_____

_____

_____

Remember, the power to transform your journey lies within your hands. Embrace the present, honor your emotions, and create a life filled with purpose, joy, and limitless possibilities. The moment is yours to seize. What will you do with it?

_____

_____

_____

_____

Exercise

Find a quiet space - Be Present.

Rising is the Root of Your Healing.

- Choose how to make this moment memorable based on your responses.

- Stay calm. Do these exercises in moderation.

- Make a memory map of your trips with your loved one.

- Put a star next to you the memories that inspired your loved one.

- How can you make one of those experiences a momentous project honoring a special day or holiday coming up?

- Pick a date and invite friends and family to celebrate their life. Make it happen, whether it's a trip to that site or a virtual celebration.

You are not extending your grief journey by making these experiences come to life. These are healing-it-forward modalities for your soul. These expressions create comforting moments during the hard moments.

Embrace the power within you to honor your grief and find solace during life's most difficult moments.

sensitivity is your superpower

Vulnerability is Bravery.

Sometimes, it feels like vulnerability is a sign of weakness.

We suppress our tears and emotions and put on a "brave" face.

But when it comes down to it, running away from vulnerability is an act of fear. We discover courage in facing vulnerability—with its raw pain, beauty, and sorrow.

Embrace the present moment without reservation. Allow your emotions to arise and create a safe space for them to heal alongside you. Make yourself at home in their company.

Journal Prompts

Close your eyes. Listen to your Inner Warrior

What steps can you take to establish a secure and nurturing environment that allows your emotions to surface and be recognized?

_____

_____

_____

_____

What is embracing vulnerability like, and how can it contribute to your healing journey?

_____

_____

_____

_____

How can you cultivate a sense of comfort and acceptance in the presence of your emotions, allowing them to guide you toward healing and growth?

_____

_____

_____

_____

How can you actively embrace vulnerability, unlock your inner strength, and create a safe space for your emotions to heal and thrive?

_____

_____

_____

_____

Exercise

Find a quiet space - Be Present.

The Pause. Take a Moment. Sit with this.

- Sit or lie down and find a quiet place to meditate.

- Consider a genuine, vulnerable emotion that best reflects your sadness. Give this feeling a name, a color, a shape, or even a face.

- Now, invite this emotion in. Make space for it in your home and life.

- Imagine yourself introducing this emotion to your loved ones. Picture it making itself at home and following you in your everyday life.

- This emotion will fade as you become more at ease. You make the most of your time together. Any unfavorable characteristics you envisioned have faded. It makes sense to develop a strong, brave side of yourself.

What are the consequences of not being vulnerable?

no Growth
no Strength
no Confidence
no Accountability
no Discernment
Always Be Mindful of Boundaries.

strength in sensitivity

The Power of Sensitivity: Embracing Your Authentic Self

Expressions like "stop being so emotional" or "don't be dramatic" are often used by people who are afraid of vulnerability. However, your sensitivity can be a source of strength, a superpower, and an authentic inner sanctuary.

It's easy to numb ourselves by getting lost in the busyness of everyday life or covering up our wounds with a band-aid. But it takes courage to face the toughest corners of our hearts. Being a strong yet vulnerable person is no small feat. It requires acknowledging our deepest emotions and deciding to heal instead of letting our wounds fester.

You possess a powerful combination of strength, sensitivity, and bravery. While letting go of the past may be challenging, choosing to heal will only make you stronger.

Journal Prompts

Our Strength is Found in the Uncomfortable Moments

Embrace your sensitivity as a source of strength. How can you harness your unique sensitivity to empower yourself and positively impact your life?

_____
_____
_____
_____

Break free from the chains of societal expectations. Challenge the notion that being emotional or dramatic is a weakness. How can you embrace and celebrate your authentic self, honoring the warrior with your emotions and experiences?

_____
_____
_____
_____

Dare to be vulnerable and dive deep into the depths of your heart. How can you summon the courage to confront and heal your inner wounds, knowing that true strength lies in embracing your vulnerabilities?

_____
_____
_____
_____

How can you actively release the past and fully embrace the healing process, allowing yourself to thrive in the present moment?

_____
_____
_____
_____

Exercise

**We are at another rebirth near ending the third stage. Take a Breath.
What a beautiful moment you've accomplished in your journey.**

- As we close our time together, I want you to take a deep breath and acknowledge where you are.

- Is it different from where you were when we first started together?

- Recognize your progress, no matter how small Embracewhere you are right now. It is enough

- Picture this very moment, strengthening your body from head to toe. Imagine this relief, presence, and 'enough-ness' washing over you. It fills you, bringing your strength, peace, and purpose.

- This moment is yours. Claim it. Tune in, heal, and OWN IT.

Unleash Your Inner Strength by Embracing Vulnerability
Don't be afraid to show your raw emotions and embrace your vulnerability. This authenticity can be empowering, and helps you to truly embark on a healing journey. Allow your emotions to guide you to a place of growth and resilience.

Thank You:
A Bow to Your Journey

Grand Rising Warrior,

Our time together has been brief, but we've already been through a lot. I sense your presence, your heart, and your optimism. Your healing journey has just begun.

I appreciate your presence and willingness to EMBRACE this moment. It's a moment meant for you, and I'm humbled to be a part of it in any way possible.

I encourage you to lean into this moment as there is great purpose, power, and presence. Remember that you deserve it all and that you are capable of achieving anything. You got this!

Stay strong and courageous,

MiMi

Michele C. Bell's narrative is a profound testament to resilience, the transformative power of embracing life's most profound challenges, and the depth of human compassion. Her journey, which began with the deeply personal and original work "*A Journey of Unconditional Love*," evolved into the 22-time award-winning story, "*A Son's Gift*," marking the inception of her distinguished career as an empathetic voice within the realm of grief literature.

With a Ph.D. in Philosophy and Metaphysics, Michele brings a unique blend of intuitive insight and scholarly depth to "*The 7 Stages of Grief* - **EMBRACE**." This work, unlike traditional grief literature, opens a space where healing is interwoven with personal growth and transformation, guided by Michele's own experiences, her profound journey through PTSD, and her scholarly insights. This journey has not only deepened her understanding of grief and resilience but also infused her writing with authenticity and compassion, offering solace and a transformative roadmap to those navigating the intricacies of loss.

Her innovative approach, blending the profound depths of intuitive philosophy with avant-garde grief counseling modalities, pioneers a novel paradigm in grief literature. Michele's work, transcending meticulous writing and exploration, charts a path towards transformative healing. Each stage, encapsulated within the evocative acronym **EMBRACE**, is meticulously crafted to guide the bereaved with dignity, offering nuanced understanding through the labyrinth of loss.

Beyond her literary contributions, Michele's life story—marked by resilience amidst adversity—enriches her professional narrative. From facing challenges such as bullying and domestic abuse to navigating the complexities of being a holistic real estate broker, Michele's experiences underscore her innate desire to support individuals through significant life transitions. The profound loss of her son to Ewings Sarcoma tested her resolve, catalyzing a shift towards mental health advocacy and the development of groundbreaking methodologies like the Soul Design technique and the *7 Stages of Grief* workbooks.

Michele's contributions extend to her active involvement in suicide prevention and domestic abuse programs, where her voice has become a force for change. Her purpose, whether as a holistic real estate broker, end-of-life expert, or mental health advocate, remains consistent—to support, guide, and uplift. As a member and keynote speaker for the **Daughters of Penelope**, Michele shares inspiring messages of healing, humor, and love, emphasizing the necessity of such virtues in today's world.

At 58, Michele C. Bell, The Grief Warrior®, stands as a testament to the enduring power of the human spirit, commanding respect and fostering deep, authentic connections. Her life experiences, granting her the invaluable CAT credentials of **Compassion, Authenticity, and Trust**, continue to inspire those fortunate enough to encounter her legacy..

Testimonial

In the wake of losing my niece, who was both an integral part of our family business and my daily life, I was engulfed by survivor's guilt and a maelstrom of emotions. At 74, having built a successful business career, I was unprepared for the profound impact this tragedy would have. The accident that took her life left me alone with my grief and a host of unresolved feelings, including an intense rage and sadness.

Then, I encountered Michele. She introduced me to a world of grace and dignity I hadn't known was possible. She guided me through techniques to stay ahead of depression, reduce stress, and embrace the present—prayer, meditation, and deep, conscious breathing became part of my routine. Her 30-day challenges and the comprehensive support she provided, spanning personal loss to business strategies, were transformative.

But Michele's impact didn't stop there. She introduced me to her eating healthy modality—incorporating balanced diets, regular exercise, and supplements into my daily regimen. These changes, under her guidance, not only improved my mental clarity but also led to significant weight loss and helped me stop drinking. Michele's approach broke me down and rebuilt me, a process my family witnessed as I underwent these massive shifts.

This woman has led me to a profound state of gratitude. Through her encouragement to write letters and share my deepest thoughts in a safe and authentic space, I found a unique kind of healing. Michele has restored joy to my life, demonstrating that even at this age, profound transformation is possible. Her expertise and genuine presence have given me back to myself, and family healthier and more vibrant. I stand in humble acknowledgment of the incredible journey she has guided me through.

Mike

DISCLAIMER

All content within the 7 Stages of Grief Alignment Workbook is original and intended solely to promote mind, body, and spirit well-being. This material does not replace the expertise or advice of a licensed mental health professional. Grief experiences are unique to each individual, and while the workbook provides supportive tools and perspectives, it does not guarantee specific outcomes. If you are experiencing intense or extreme distress, please consult a professional.

By using this course, you acknowledge and accept these terms and conditions. The 7 Stages of Grief certification program, conceived and developed by Dr. Michele Bell, offers an innovative, holistic, and empathy-driven approach to understanding and navigating grief. It is rooted in comprehensive research and deep insight into the human experience of loss and recovery.

Program Overview:
- Embracing Growth in Grief: Recognize the transformative potential within grief.
- The 7 Stages of Grief: Explore the intricate emotional journey of grief, encompassing its multifaceted seven stages.
- Pivoting with Purpose: Equip yourself with practical tools to channel grief's raw energy into purposeful action.
- Understanding the Power of Resistance: Gain insights into the obstacles resistance can pose on the healing journey and learn strategies to address and overcome it.
- Coping Modalities: Discover and apply various coping methods tailored to individual grief journeys or to assist others on this path.
- Certification: As a culmination, the program offers a certification examination to ensure a comprehensive understanding of the 7 Stages of Grief methodology.

Engage with the 7 Stages of Grief, All-In-One Master Compilation program to acquire a compassionate and informed approach to navigating the intricate labyrinth of grief, whether for personal growth or as a professional commitment.

Remember, every voice matters in bringing light to the shadows of grief. By uniting, we can raise awareness and create a world where everyone feels understood and supported during their moments of profound loss. I deeply appreciate your commitment to this cause. Please take a moment to sign the **Loss Awareness Day** petition on **Change.org**, inspired by the heartfelt endeavors of Lisa Marie Presley. Together, we can make a difference.
With heartfelt gratitude and hope,
MiMi + The Grief Warrior®

www.ingramcontent.com/pod-product-compliance
Lightning Source LLC
Chambersburg PA
CBHW041151120626
46547CB00020B/3190